by Ellen Lawrence

Consultants:

Suzy Gazlay, MA
Recipient, Presidential Award for Excellence in Science Teaching

Kimberly Brenneman, PhD
National Institute for Early Education Research, Rutgers University, New Brunswick, New Jersey

BEARPORT
PUBLISHING

New York, New York

Credits

Cover, © LianeM/Shutterstock, © Zadiraka Evgenii/Shutterstock, and © Vitaly Korovin/Shutterstock; 2–3, © CoraMax/Shutterstock, © Richard Petersen/Shutterstock, and © Valentina Razumova; 4–5, © Club4traveler/Shutterstock, © Be Good/Shutterstock, © Konstantin L/Shutterstock, © Rafal Olechowski/Shutterstock, © LeS/Shutterstock, © BlueOrange Studio/Shutterstock, and © Levranii/Shutterstock; 6–7, © CoraMax/Shutterstock, © Richard Petersen/Shutterstock, © Maxim Ibragimov/Shutterstock, and © Scisetti Alfio/Shutterstock; 8–9, © CoraMax/Shutterstock, © J. Palys/Shutterstock, © Richard Petersen/Shutterstock, © Sarah Marchant/Shutterstock, © warnsweet/Shutterstock, © vadimmmus/Shutterstock, © Imageman/Shutterstock, and © Ruby Tuesday Books; 10–11, © CoraMax/Shutterstock, © pixavril/Shutterstock, © Biehler Michael/Shutterstock, and © JGA/Shutterstock; 12–13, © CoraMax/Shutterstock, © endeavour/Shutterstock, © Joe Belanger/Shutterstock, and © JGA/Shutterstock; 14–15, © CoraMax/Shutterstock, © Ruby Tuesday Books, and © TigerForce/Shutterstock; 16–17, © CoraMax/Shutterstock, © Ruby Tuesday Books, © elenaburn/Shutterstock, © zhekoss/Shutterstock, © stocksolutions/Shutterstock, and © Artography/Shutterstock; 18–19, © CoraMax/Shutterstock and © Igor Karasi/Shutterstock; 20–21, © CoraMax/Shutterstock and © Ruby Tuesday Books; 22, © Tu Le/Shutterstock, © Siim Sepp/Shutterstock, © farbled/Shutterstock, and © isabela66/Shutterstock; 23, © kojihirano/Shutterstock, © Rudchenko Lillia/Shutterstock, © kamira/Shutterstock, © Richard Petersen/Shutterstock, © maxim ibragimov/Shutterstock, and © Marko Poplasen/Shutterstock.

Publisher: Kenn Goin
Senior Editor: Joyce Tavolacci
Creative Director: Spencer Brinker
Design: Emma Randall
Photo Researcher: Ruby Tuesday Books Ltd.

Library of Congress Cataloging-in-Publication Data

Lawrence, Ellen, 1967– author.
  Rocks & minerals / by Ellen Lawrence ; consultants: Suzy Gazlay, MA, Recipient, Presidential Award for Excellence in Science Teaching, Kimberly Brenneman, PhD, National Institute for Early Education Research, Rutgers University, New Brunswick, New Jersey.
     pages cm. — (FUN-damental experiments)
  Includes bibliographical references and index.
  ISBN 978-1-62724-540-1 (library binding) — ISBN 1-62724-540-5 (library binding)
 1. Rocks—Juvenile literature. 2. Minerals—Juvenile literature. 3. Petrology—Juvenile literature. I. Title. II. Title: Rocks and minerals. III. Series: Lawrence, Ellen, 1967– FUN-damental experiments.
  QE432.2.L393 2015
  552—dc23
                              2014040636

For more information, write to Bearport Publishing Company, Inc., 45 West 21st Street, Suite 3B, New York, NY 10010. Printed in the United States of America.

10 9 8 7 6 5 4 3 2 1

Contents

Let's Investigate Rocks and Minerals

Rocks are everywhere. You can find them in many different places—in a backyard, in a garden, at the foot of a mountain, or at the beach. Yet no matter where they come from or how different they look, all rocks are made up of solid substances called **minerals**. Inside this book are lots of fun experiments about rocks and minerals. So grab a notebook, and let's start investigating!

Check It Out!

Tall mountains, deep **canyons**, and steep cliffs are all made of rock. Different things you see in towns and cities, such as buildings, may be made of rock, too. In fact, you probably see rock every day—sometimes without even knowing it!

In your notebook, make a list of all the places you see rock. Answer the following questions and write down the things you observe about the rocks you've spotted.

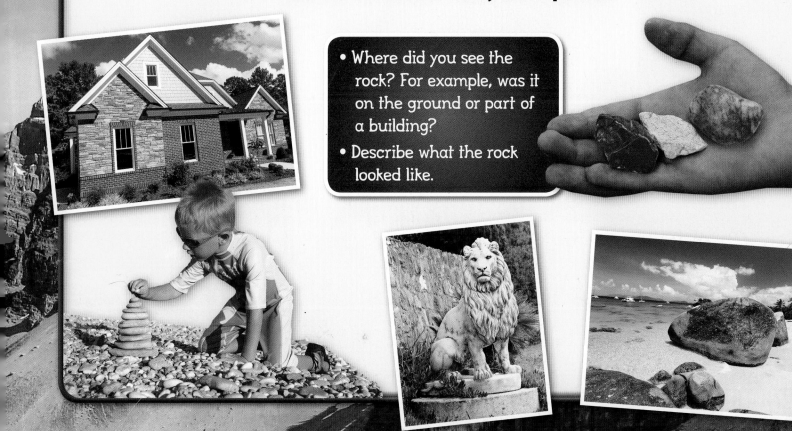

- Where did you see the rock? For example, was it on the ground or part of a building?
- Describe what the rock looked like.

Are all rocks the same?

In this first investigation, you will collect rocks. Then you will closely examine them to observe their different **properties**—just like a scientist called a **geologist** would. Let's investigate to find out if all rocks are the same.

You will need:

- Six rocks (about the size of ping-pong balls)
- A black marker
- A magnifying glass
- A notebook and pencil

 Find six rocks. You can look for rocks in a backyard, or park, or at the beach.

 Place the six rocks on a table. Use a marker to label them 1 to 6.

Examine the first rock. Use the magnifying glass to get an up close look. Think about the following questions.

▶ What words describe the feel of your rock? For example, is it rough, crumbly, smooth, or sharp?

▶ What shape is the rock?

▶ What colors do you see in the rock?

▶ Is the rock shiny or dull?

▶ What do you see when you look at the rock with a magnifying glass?

 Draw a chart like this in your notebook. Then record everything you observed about the rock in the chart.

Rocks examined	How does it feel?	Shape	Colors	Shiny or dull?	What I can see with a magnifying glass
Rock 1					
Rock 2					
Rock 3					
Rock 4					
Rock 5					
Rock 6					

 Now examine the other five rocks and record your observations in the chart.

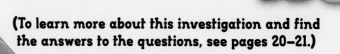

▶ In what ways are the rocks similar to one another?

▶ In what ways are they different?

(To learn more about this investigation and find the answers to the questions, see pages 20–21.)

What are rocks made of?

feldspar

quartz

Not all rocks look the same. If you looked at a rock under a **microscope**, you would see that it is made of tiny grains of minerals. Minerals form naturally on Earth. Some examples of minerals are feldspar, quartz, and metals such as iron and gold. Minerals make rocks look different. Let's investigate!

1 Place a cup of each of the dried goods on a table. These items will take the place of minerals in this experiment.

2 Choose 30 pieces from your selection of pretend minerals and put them in a bowl.

You will need:

- A measuring cup
- At least four dried food items, such as pasta, rice, beans, and lentils
- A small bowl
- A spoon
- White glue
- A sheet of wax paper
- A notebook and pencil
- Two rocks

Add a spoonful of glue to the bowl and mix it with the pretend minerals. Keep adding small amounts of glue until all the pieces are stuck together in a lumpy blob.

 Place the blob on a sheet of wax paper and leave it to dry. You have made a pretend rock with the pretend minerals.

 Collect 30 new pieces from your selection of minerals to form a different combination.

▶ **Do you think these minerals will make a rock that looks the same as or different from the first rock? Why?**

Write down your **predictions** in your notebook.

Then make the second rock and leave it to dry.

In your notebook, record everything that happened.

▶ **In what ways are the two pretend rocks the same? In what ways are they different?**

▶ **Now look at two real rocks. Why do you think the two real rocks look different from one another?**

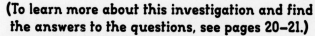
(To learn more about this investigation and find the answers to the questions, see pages 20–21.)

9

How do big rocks become little rocks?

Over millions of years, big rocks break apart. How does this happen? One substance that can break rocks apart is water. Let's investigate one way that water can turn big rocks into little rocks.

You will need:

- Measuring cups
- ½ cup of flour
- ¼ cup of salt
- A mixing bowl
- ¼ cup of water
- A spoon
- A rolling pin
- A ruler
- An adult helper
- A balloon
- A notebook and pencil

 In this investigation, you will make a special dough that will become your pretend rock. Put the flour and salt into the mixing bowl. Add some of the water, and mix everything with the spoon. Keep adding water and mixing with the spoon and your hands until you have made dough.

 Place the dough on a kitchen countertop. Use a rolling pin or your hands to flatten the dough until it's about ¼ inch (0.6 cm) thick.

3 Ask an adult helper to stretch the opening of the balloon over a faucet. Then slowly fill the balloon with water until it's the size of a ping-pong ball. Remove the balloon from the faucet, squeeze out all the air, and tie the end.

4 Place the water-filled balloon in the center of the dough. Wrap the dough around the balloon so the balloon is completely covered.

5 Leave your dough ball in a warm place for about two days, until it dries and turns hard. Now it has become a pretend rock. Put it in the freezer overnight.

▶ What do you think will happen to the water inside the balloon?

▶ What do you think the water will do to the rock?

Write your predictions in your notebook.

In the morning, take your rock out of the freezer.

In your notebook, record everything that happened.

▶ What has happened to the rock?

▶ What has happened to the water?

▶ What do you think the water has done to the rock?

(To learn more about this investigation and find the answers to the questions, see pages 20–21.)

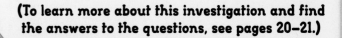

11

How does wind change rocks?

When water turns to ice and breaks rocks apart, it's called **weathering**. Just like water and ice, wind can also weather rocks. In this next investigation, let's find out how wind can change rocks.

You will need:

- Measuring cups
- ½ cup of flour
- ¼ cup of salt
- A mixing bowl
- ¼ cup of water
- A spoon
- A notebook and pencil
- A piece of sandpaper
- A piece of black construction paper

1 Begin by making a pretend rock. Put the flour and salt into the mixing bowl. Add some of the water. Mix with the spoon. Keep adding water and mixing until you have made dough.

Form your dough into a rock shape. Leave the dough rock in a warm place for about two days, until it dries and becomes hard. To dry it faster, place it in a sunny spot or next to a warm radiator.

▶ **What does the surface of your pretend rock feel like?**

▶ **What do you think will happen to your rock if you rub it with some sandpaper?**

Write your observations and predictions in your notebook.

 Hold your rock over the black construction paper. Rub the sandpaper over the rock in one spot for about a minute.

▶ **Touch the surface of the rock where you've been rubbing. How does it feel?**

▶ **What else has happened to your rock?**

In your notebook, record everything that happened.

▶ **How do you think the wind can act like sandpaper?**

(To learn more about this investigation and find the answers to the questions, see pages 20–21.)

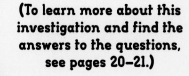

How do rough rocks become smooth?

You found out that the wind can make a rough rock smooth. There's also another way that rough rocks can become smooth and rounded. Grab your notebook, and let's investigate!

You will need:

- Two thick sticks of sidewalk chalk
- A notebook and pencil
- An empty glass jar with a tight-fitting lid
- Water
- A spoon

 Snap each piece of sidewalk chalk into two small chunks that are each about 2 inches (5 cm) long.

 Examine the pieces of chalk.

▶ **What shape are they?**

▶ **Do they have any flat areas or rough edges?**

Write your observations in your notebook.

Place the four chunks of chalk into the jar. Pour in enough water to cover the chalk. Screw on the lid tightly.

▶ **What do you think will happen to the chalk if you shake the jar?**

▶ **Do you think the shape of the chalk pieces will change or stay the same?**

Write your predictions in your notebook.

 Shake the jar hard as you count to 100. Give your arms a short rest. Then shake the jar again while counting to 100.

 Scoop the chalk chunks out of the jar with a spoon.

▶ **How have they changed?**

▶ **What do you think has happened to them?**

In your notebook, write down everything you observed.

▶ You shook the chalk pieces in water and changed their shape. How and where do you think this might happen to real rocks?

(To learn more about this investigation and find the answers to the questions, see pages 20–21.)

Why do some rocks have stripes?

sedimentary rock

Some rocks have colorful stripes, or layers, that are made from tiny pieces of rock called **sediment**. These rocks belong to a group called sedimentary rocks. When wind and water weather big rocks, sediment breaks off. So how do these pieces form sedimentary rock? Let's find out! Be sure to wash your hands before you begin so you can eat your experiment at the end!

You will need:

- An adult helper
- A knife
- A slice of white bread
- A slice of whole-wheat bread
- A plate
- Peanut butter
- Jelly or jam
- A handful of raisins (or another type of small dried fruit)
- A handful of dry cereal

1 Ask an adult helper to cut the two slices of bread into quarters on a plate. You will now have eight small pieces of bread.

Spread a layer of peanut butter and a layer of jelly on one of the pieces of bread.

 Add another piece of bread. Then add a layer of jelly. Keep adding layers of bread, jelly, peanut butter, raisins, and cereal. Finish up by putting the eighth piece of bread on top of your sandwich.

 Push down on your sandwich with your clean hands. Then ask your adult helper to carefully cut the sandwich in half. Now look at the inside of the sandwich.

▶ **What do you see?**

▶ **What has happened to all the different ingredients?**

Look at this picture of a sedimentary rock. Compare it to the inside of your sandwich.

▶ **How are the rock and the sandwich alike?**

▶ **Why do you think the rock has different-colored layers?**

(To learn more about this investigation and find the answers to the questions, see pages 20–21.)

How did dinosaurs leave footprints in rock?

Sometimes scientists find rocks with footprints in them that were made by dinosaurs that lived millions of years ago. Look at the photo of a dinosaur footprint. How do you think the footprint got left in the hard, solid rock? Let's investigate!

You will need:

- Measuring cups
- ½ cup of flour
- ¼ cup of salt
- A mixing bowl
- 1 cup of cold coffee or tea
- A spoon
- A sheet of wax paper
- A ruler
- A notebook and pencil

 Make pretend mud by putting the flour and salt into the mixing bowl. Then add a little of the cold coffee or tea and stir with the spoon. Keep adding small amounts of liquid until the mixture is smooth and thick.

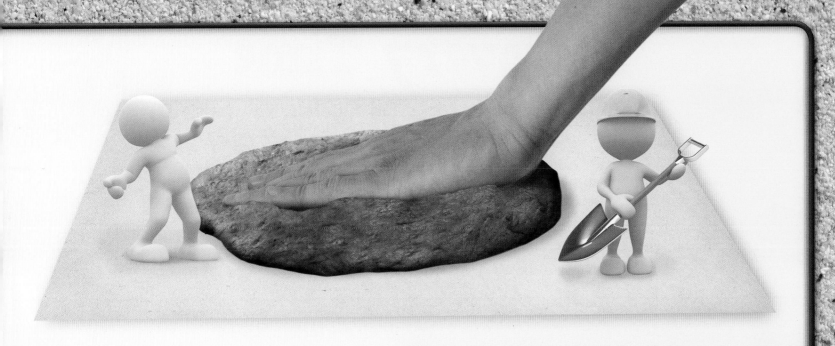

 Scoop the mixture onto the wax paper and smooth it out until it's about 1 inch (2.5 cm) thick.

 Press your hand into the rock mixture and make a handprint. Now leave the mixture in a warm place for about two days, until it dries and turns hard like a rock. To dry it faster, place it in a sunny spot or next to a warm radiator.

In your notebook, record everything that happened.

▶ What happened to the muddy mixture?

▶ What happened to your handprint?

▶ Now that you've tried this experiment, how do you think it's possible for dinosaur footprints to be in solid rock?

(To learn more about this investigation and find the answers to the questions, see pages 20–21.)

Discovery Time

It's fun to learn about rocks and minerals. Now let's check out all the exciting things we've discovered.

Pages 6–7

Are all rocks the same?

All rocks are not the same. Rocks come in many different colors, shapes, and textures. Sometimes, when you examine two rocks, they will have properties that are the same and properties that are different. For example, the two rocks might both be dull and smooth. However, one rock might be brown and flat, while the other rock is black and round.

Pages 8–9

What are rocks made of?

The two pretend rocks were similar in appearance, yet they still looked different. That's because even though they were made of the same pretend minerals, or ingredients, each rock was made from a different combination of ingredients. This is what happens with real rock, too. Grains of minerals join together to make solid rock. Different combinations of minerals make rocks that look different.

Pages 10–11

How do big rocks become little rocks?

The water inside the balloon froze. When water turns to ice, it expands, or takes up more space. As the ice expanded, it pushed against the dough rock and made it crack. This is exactly what happens to real rocks. Water from rain or melted snow trickles into cracks in big rocks. If the temperature gets cold enough, the water freezes. As the water turns to ice, the ice expands and pushes the crack open. As the rock splits, pieces break off.

How does wind change rocks?

When you rubbed the sandpaper on the pretend rock, tiny pieces of the rock broke off. This made the rock's surface smoother. This is exactly what happens to real rocks when the wind blows. Wind picks up loose pieces of sand or dirt. Then the force of the wind rubs the flying sand or dirt against large rocks and causes tiny pieces of rock to break off. When wind blows over rocks, it can also make them smoother. In the experiment, your hand acted like the wind and the sandpaper acted like sand or dirt carried by the wind.

How do rough rocks become smooth?

As you shook the jar of water, the chalk rocks bumped and crashed into each other. This caused tiny bits of chalk to break off. After lots of shaking, the chalk rocks changed shape. They became smooth and rounded. This is what happens to real rocks in water. Sometimes small rocks break off from a cliff and fall into the sea or a river. The rocks are smashed against each other by rough waves or rushing water until they become smooth and rounded.

Why do some rocks have stripes?

The layers in sedimentary rock are made of different kinds of sediment, just like the layers in your sandwich are made of different ingredients. Layers of sediment build up on top of each other. Sometimes this happens in water, such as in a lake. Sediment gets washed into the lake by a river and settles at the bottom. Layer after layer builds up. The layers get heavier and press together (just like your hand pressed on your sandwich) as more layers are added. Over millions of years, the layers of sediment join together and become solid rock.

How did dinosaurs leave footprints in rock?

The muddy mixture turned hard like a rock. Your handprint also became part of the pretend rock. Millions of years ago, dinosaurs made footprints in soft mud. Over time, the mud dried, hardened, and became rock. The dinosaur footprints dried, too, and became part of the solid rock.

21

Rocks and Minerals in Your World

You've discovered a lot about rocks and minerals. Now check out some more of Earth's amazing rocks and minerals.

1. This rock is called The Wave. It is in a desert in Arizona.

▶ **How do you think the rock got its smooth, wavelike shape?**

2. This rock contains a mineral called graphite. People use this grayish-black mineral for writing.

▶ **What object can you write with that contains graphite?**

3. This rock contains a shiny, yellow-colored mineral.

▶ **What do you think the mineral is?**

4. On a beach, there may be large rocks, small pebbles, and sand.

▶ **What do you think sand is made of?**

Answers: **1.** The Wave was once a huge rough rock. Over millions of years, swirling dusty winds weathered the rock, and tiny pieces broke off. The swirling dust carved the rock's wavelike shape and made the rock smooth. **2.** A pencil—graphite is used to make the dark grayish-black part of a pencil that writes. **3.** The mineral is gold—a metal that people use to make jewelry and other objects. **4.** Each grain of sand on a beach is a tiny piece of rock. Ocean waves smash into cliffs and into larger rocks, breaking off tiny pieces that become sand.

Science Words

canyons (KAN-yuhnz) steep-walled valleys carved out by rivers

geologist (jee-OL-uh-jist) a scientist who studies rocks

microscope (MYE-kruh-skohp) a tool or machine used to see things that are too small to see with the eyes alone

minerals (MIN-ur-uhlz) the solid substances found in nature that make up rocks; quartz, feldspar, and gold are all minerals

predictions (pri-DIK-shuhnz) guesses that something will happen in a certain way; they are often based on facts a person knows or something a person has observed

properties (PROP-ur-teez) things you can notice about an object or substance using your senses

sediment (SED-uh-muhnt) tiny pieces of rock that have broken away from larger rocks; pebbles and grains of sand are both types of sediment

weathering (WETH-ur-ing) the wearing away or breaking up of large rocks by water, snow, ice, and wind to make sediment

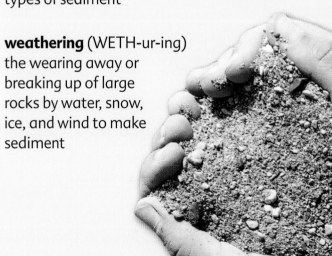

Index

Read More

Lawrence, Ellen. *What Is the Rock Cycle? (Rock-ology).* New York: Bearport (2015).

Owen, Ruth. *Science and Craft Projects with Rocks and Soil (Get Crafty Outdoors).* New York: PowerKids Press (2013).

Zoehfeld, Kathleen Weidner. *Rocks and Minerals.* Washington, DC: National Geographic (2012).

Learn More Online

To learn more about rocks and minerals, visit
www.bearportpublishing.com/FundamentalExperiments

About the Author

Ellen Lawrence lives in the United Kingdom. Her favorite books to write are those about nature and animals. In fact, the first book Ellen bought for herself, when she was six years old, was the story of a gorilla named Patty Cake that was born in New York's Central Park Zoo.